Accelerated Millionaire: The Ultimate Guide to Rapid Wealth Accumulation

By Casey Kroon

Table of Contents

Accelerated Millionaire:
The Ultimate Guide to Rapid Wealth Accumulation

Chapter 1: The Mindset of a Millionaire
- Introduction to the mindset shift required to achieve millionaire status quickly.
- Cultivating a mindset of abundance, determination, and strategic thinking.
- Techniques for overcoming limiting beliefs and embracing a wealth-focused mentality.

Chapter 2: Leveraging Technology for Financial Growth
- Harnessing the power of emerging technologies to streamline wealth generation.
- Utilizing automation, artificial intelligence, and algorithms to optimize investment strategies.
- Exploring cryptocurrency, blockchain, and decentralized finance (DeFi) for exponential growth opportunities.

Chapter 3: Strategic Investments and Income Generation
- Understanding the principles of strategic investing in diverse asset classes.
- Identifying high-potential investment opportunities in stocks, real estate, and startups.
- Implementing income-generating strategies such as passive income streams, affiliate marketing, and   digital entrepreneurship.

Chapter 4: Networking and Collaboration for Success
- Building a powerful network of mentors, advisors, and collaborators.
- Leveraging social capital for access to opportunities, resources, and knowledge.
- Establishing mutually beneficial partnerships and alliances to accelerate wealth creation.

Chapter 5: Risk Management and Resilience
- Developing a robust risk management strategy to safeguard wealth and minimize losses.
- Diversifying investments and maintaining a balanced portfolio.
- Cultivating resilience and adaptability to navigate market fluctuations and economic challenges.

Chapter 6: Continuous Learning and Growth
- Embracing a lifelong learning mindset to stay ahead in an ever-evolving landscape.
- Investing in personal and professional development to enhance skills and knowledge.
- Leveraging online courses, workshops, and mentorship programs for continuous growth and improvement.

Chapter 7: Giving Back and Impactful Philanthropy
- Recognizing the importance of giving back to society and making a positive impact.
- Incorporating philanthropy into wealth-building strategies for long-term fulfillment and legacy.
- Supporting causes aligned with personal values and contributing to meaningful social change.

Chapter 8: Scaling Success and Multiplying Impact
- Scaling successful ventures and expanding wealth-building strategies for exponential growth.
- Multiplying impact through innovative business models, investments, and philanthropic initiatives.
- Empowering others to achieve financial independence and become millionaires through education, mentorship, and empowerment.

Conclusion: Empowering the Masses to Millionaire Status
- Recap of key strategies and principles for rapid wealth accumulation.
- Encouragement to take action, persevere, and seize opportunities for financial success.
- Vision for a future where millions of individuals worldwide achieve millionaire status and create a legacy of abundance and prosperity.

Authors Words:

As the author of "Accelerated Millionaire: The Ultimate Guide to Rapid Wealth," I embarked on this writing journey fueled by a deep passion for empowering individuals to achieve financial freedom and abundance. Drawing upon years of experience in finance, entrepreneurship, and personal development, I have dedicated myself to distilling the most effective wealth-building strategies into this comprehensive guide.

Over the course of many years, I have immersed myself in the world of finance, continually seeking knowledge, honing my skills, and navigating the ever-evolving landscape of wealth creation. Through countless hours of research, experimentation, and real-world experience, I have gained invaluable insights and discovered the principles that truly accelerate the path to millionaire status.

"Accelerated Millionaire" is the culmination of this journey—a culmination of years of dedication, hard work, and relentless pursuit of excellence. Within its pages, you will find a treasure trove of wisdom, strategies, and practical advice that will revolutionize your approach to wealth-building and empower you to achieve your financial goals with unprecedented speed and efficiency.

Whether you're a seasoned investor, aspiring entrepreneur, or simply someone with a burning desire to transform your financial future, "Accelerated Millionaire" is your ultimate guide to success. It is my sincerest hope that this book will serve as a catalyst for positive change in your life, propelling you towards greater prosperity, abundance, and fulfillment. Prepare to embark on a transformative journey—one that will forever change the trajectory of your financial destiny.

Special Thank you to my dad,

Dick Kroon,

For never giving up on my well being and prospering an unwavering quest for truth and richness of life and soul.

I love you beyond words can express.

Chapter 1

The Mindset of a Millionaire

Introduction:

Achieving millionaire status is not just about accumulating wealth; it requires a fundamental shift in mindset. In this chapter, we will explore the essential components of the millionaire mindset and how to cultivate it to accelerate your path to financial success. By adopting the mindset of a millionaire, you will unlock the potential to attract abundance, maintain unwavering determination, and employ strategic thinking to achieve your goals.

Cultivating a Mindset of Abundance:

The first step in cultivating a millionaire mindset is to embrace the principle of abundance. Instead of viewing the world through a lens of scarcity and limitation, millionaires see opportunities everywhere. They understand that there is more than enough wealth to go around and believe in their ability to create abundance in their own lives and the lives of others.

To cultivate a mindset of abundance, it's essential

to practice gratitude daily. Gratitude shifts your focus from what you lack to what you have, creating a positive mindset that attracts more abundance into your life.

Start each day by acknowledging and appreciating the blessings in your life, whether it's your health, relationships, or opportunities for growth.

Additionally, surround yourself with positivity by consuming uplifting content, associating with optimistic individuals, and visualizing your desired outcomes. By immersing yourself in an environment of abundance, you will train your mind to see possibilities where others see obstacles.

Determination:

Determination is the fuel that drives millionaires to overcome challenges and persist in the pursuit of their goals. It's the unwavering commitment to success, even in the face of adversity. To develop a millionaire's level of determination, you must first clarify your vision and set specific, measurable goals.

Create a compelling vision of your ideal life and the wealth you desire to achieve. Visualize yourself living that life with vivid detail, engaging all your senses to make it feel real. Then, break down your vision into actionable goals with clear deadlines and milestones.

Next, develop resilience by reframing failures as learning opportunities and maintaining a growth mindset. Understand that setbacks are inevitable on the path to success, but they do not define you. Instead, view them as valuable feedback that propels you closer to your goals.

Finally, cultivate discipline and consistency by establishing daily habits that align with your goals. Success is not the result of sporadic bursts of effort but rather the culmination of small, consistent actions over time. By staying focused and disciplined, you will overcome obstacles and achieve remarkable results.

Strategic Thinking:
Strategic thinking is the hallmark of the millionaire mindset, enabling individuals to make informed decisions and maximize opportunities for wealth creation. It involves analyzing situations critically, identifying potential risks and rewards, and devising a plan of action to achieve desired outcomes.

To develop strategic thinking skills, cultivate

curiosity and a hunger for knowledge. Stay informed about current events, market trends, and emerging technologies that could impact your financial endeavors. Continuously seek out new perspectives and insights to broaden your understanding of the world and uncover innovative solutions to complex problems.

Additionally, practice strategic goal setting by prioritizing tasks based on their impact and feasibility. Focus your energy on high-leverage activities that move you closer to your goals while delegating or eliminating tasks that do not align with your objectives.

Finally, embrace flexibility and adaptability in your approach to achieving wealth. Recognize that the path to success is not always linear and be willing to pivot when circumstances change. By remaining agile and open-minded, you will seize opportunities as they arise and stay ahead of the curve in an ever-evolving landscape.

Techniques for Overcoming Limiting Beliefs:

One of the most significant barriers to achieving millionaire status is the presence of limiting beliefs—deep-seated beliefs about yourself and your capabilities that hold you back from reaching your full potential. These beliefs often stem from past experiences, societal conditioning, or negative self-talk.

To overcome limiting beliefs, start by identifying and challenging them head-on. Ask yourself: What beliefs do I hold about money, success, and wealth? Are these beliefs serving me or holding me back? Reframe negative beliefs into empowering affirmations that affirm your worthiness and potential for success.

Next, surround yourself with positive influences that reinforce your belief in yourself and your ability to achieve greatness. Seek out mentors, coaches, and role models who have achieved the level of success you aspire to and learn from their experiences.

Finally, take bold action in the face of fear and uncertainty. Break out of your comfort zone and confront your fears head-on, knowing that growth and transformation lie on the other side of discomfort. By challenging your limiting beliefs and stepping into your power, you will unlock new levels of success and abundance in your life.

Conclusion:

Cultivating the mindset of a millionaire is not an overnight transformation but a lifelong journey of growth and self-discovery. By embracing abundance, determination, strategic thinking, and techniques for overcoming limiting beliefs, you will unlock the keys to rapid wealth accumulation and create a life of abundance and fulfillment beyond your wildest dreams.

Chapter 2

Leveraging Technology for Financial Growth

Harnessing the Power of Emerging Technologies:

In today's digital age, advancements in technology have revolutionized the way we manage and grow our finances. From automation to artificial intelligence, emerging technologies offer unprecedented opportunities to streamline wealth generation and maximize returns on investments.

Automation has become a cornerstone of modern finance, allowing investors to execute trades, rebalance portfolios, and manage their finances with unprecedented efficiency. By automating routine tasks and processes, investors can free up time to focus on strategic decision-making and wealth-building activities.

Artificial intelligence (AI) and machine learning algorithms are transforming the investment landscape by analyzing vast amounts of data to identify patterns, trends, and opportunities that human investors may overlook. These technologies can analyze market sentiment, predict price movements, and optimize investment strategies in real-time, providing investors with a competitive edge in the market.

Utilizing Automation, Artificial Intelligence, and Algorithms to Optimize Investment Strategies:

One of the key benefits of leveraging technology in finance is the ability to optimize investment strategies for maximum returns. AI-powered algorithms can analyze historical data, market trends, and economic indicators to identify high-potential investment opportunities and allocate capital accordingly.

Robo-advisors, for example, use algorithms to create and manage diversified investment portfolios tailored to investors' risk tolerance, financial goals, and time horizon. These platforms offer low-cost, automated investment management services that provide access to sophisticated investment strategies previously reserved for high-net-worth individuals.

Additionally, algorithmic trading, also known as automated trading or black-box trading, allows investors to execute trades at lightning speed based on pre-defined criteria and market conditions. These algorithms can identify arbitrage opportunities, execute trades with precision timing, and mitigate risks in volatile markets, resulting in potentially higher returns and reduced trading costs.

Exploring Cryptocurrency, Blockchain, and Decentralized Finance (DeFi) for Exponential Growth Opportunities:

Cryptocurrency, blockchain technology, and decentralized finance (DeFi) represent some of the most disruptive innovations in finance today, offering unparalleled opportunities for exponential growth and wealth creation.

Cryptocurrency, such as Bitcoin and Ethereum, has gained widespread adoption as a store of value, medium of exchange, and investment asset. The decentralized nature of cryptocurrencies eliminates the need for intermediaries such as banks or governments, allowing for peer-to-peer transactions with lower fees and greater transparency.

Blockchain technology, the underlying technology behind cryptocurrencies, has applications beyond digital currencies, including supply chain management, identity verification, and asset tokenization. By leveraging blockchain technology, investors can streamline processes, reduce fraud, and unlock new revenue streams in various industries.

Decentralized finance (DeFi) platforms are leveraging blockchain technology to create open, permissionless financial systems that enable peer-to-peer lending, borrowing, trading, and asset management without intermediaries. These platforms offer higher yields, lower fees, and greater accessibility compared to traditional financial services, democratizing access to financial products and services for individuals worldwide.

In summary, by harnessing the power of emerging technologies such as automation, artificial intelligence, cryptocurrency, blockchain, and decentralized finance, investors can streamline wealth generation, optimize investment strategies, and unlock exponential growth opportunities in today's rapidly evolving financial landscape.

Chapter 3: Strategic Investments and Income Generation

Understanding the Principles of Strategic Investing in Diverse Asset Classes:

Strategic investing is the process of allocating capital across various asset classes to achieve long-term financial goals while managing risk. Diversification is a fundamental principle of strategic investing, as it helps spread risk and optimize returns by investing in assets with low correlation to one another.

Asset classes commonly utilized in strategic investing include:
- Stocks: Ownership stakes in publicly traded companies that offer the potential for capital appreciation and dividend income.
- Bonds: Fixed-income securities issued by governments, corporations, or municipalities that provide regular interest payments and return of principal at maturity.
- Real Estate: Physical properties such as residential, commercial, or industrial real estate that generate rental income and potential for property appreciation.

- Commodities: Raw materials or primary agricultural products such as gold, oil, and agricultural products that serve as a hedge against inflation and geopolitical risks.
- Alternative Investments: Hedge funds, private equity, venture capital, and other alternative investments that offer diversification benefits and potentially higher returns but also higher risk.

Identifying High-Potential Investment Opportunities:

Successful investors employ a variety of strategies to identify high-potential investment opportunities across different asset classes.

In stocks, investors may use fundamental analysis to evaluate the financial health and growth prospects of companies, technical analysis to analyze price trends and patterns, and quantitative analysis to assess historical data and identify trading signals.

In real estate, investors may research local market trends, demographics, and economic indicators to identify undervalued properties with potential for rental income and capital appreciation. They may also explore crowdfunding platforms or real estate investment trusts (REITs) for diversified exposure to real estate assets.

In startups, investors may conduct due diligence on entrepreneurs, market opportunity, competitive landscape, and business model to assess the potential for growth and scalability. They may also leverage angel investor networks, venture capital firms, or online platforms to discover investment opportunities in early-stage companies.

Implementing Income-Generating Strategies:

Passive income streams are essential for achieving financial independence and generating ongoing cash flow without active involvement. Common passive income strategies include:
- **Rental Properties:** Owning and renting out residential or commercial real estate properties to generate rental income.
- **Dividend Stocks:** Investing in stocks of companies that pay regular dividends to shareholders.
- **Peer-to-Peer Lending:** Providing loans to individuals or businesses through online lending platforms in exchange for interest payments.
- **Affiliate Marketing:** Promoting products or services through affiliate links & earning commissions on sales generated through your referrals.
- **Digital Entrepreneurship:** Creating and monetizing digital products or services such as e-books, online courses, software applications, or membership sites.

By strategically allocating capital across diverse asset classes, identifying high-potential investment opportunities, and implementing income-generating strategies, investors can build wealth and achieve financial freedom over time. However, it's essential to conduct thorough research, seek professional advice when necessary, and continually monitor and adjust your investment portfolio to align with your financial goals and risk tolerance.

Chapter 4: Networking and Collaboration for Success

Building a Powerful Network of Mentors, Advisors, and Collaborators:

Networking is a crucial component of success in any field, including finance and entrepreneurship. By surrounding yourself with mentors, advisors, and collaborators who possess knowledge, experience, and connections, you can accelerate your learning, avoid costly mistakes, and unlock new opportunities for growth and advancement.

To build a powerful network, start by identifying individuals who have achieved success in your desired field or industry. Reach out to them with a genuine interest in learning from their experiences and insights. Offer value in return by volunteering your time, expertise, or assistance on projects or initiatives that align with their goals and interests.

Attend industry events, conferences, and networking mixers to expand your circle of contacts and connect with like-minded professionals. Join professional associations, alumni networks, and online communities to access a wealth of resources, educational opportunities, and networking events.

Leveraging Social Capital for Access to Opportunities, Resources, and Knowledge:
Social capital refers to the network of relationships and connections that individuals can leverage to gain access to valuable opportunities, resources, and knowledge. By nurturing and expanding your social capital, you can increase your visibility, credibility, and influence within your industry or community.

To leverage social capital effectively, focus on building authentic relationships based on trust, reciprocity, and mutual respect. Be genuinely interested in others' success and willing to offer support, guidance, and resources whenever possible.

Engage in networking activities such as informational interviews, coffee meetings, and networking events to deepen connections and expand your network. Follow up with contacts regularly to maintain relationships and stay top-of-mind for potential opportunities.

Additionally, actively participate in online communities, forums, and social media platforms relevant to your industry or interests. Share valuable insights, contribute to discussions, and offer assistance to others to establish yourself as a thought leader and valuable resource within your network.

Establishing Mutually Beneficial Partnerships and Alliances to Accelerate Wealth Creation:

Partnerships and alliances can be powerful vehicles for accelerating wealth creation by leveraging complementary strengths, resources, and networks. By collaborating with strategic partners, you can access new markets, expand your reach, and create synergies that benefit all parties involved.

When seeking potential partners, look for individuals or organizations with complementary skills, expertise, or resources that align with your goals and objectives. Consider how each partner can contribute value to the partnership and how you can reciprocate in return.

Negotiate mutually beneficial agreements that outline clear roles, responsibilities, and expectations for each party involved. Be transparent and communicate openly to build trust and ensure alignment throughout the partnership.

Regularly evaluate and assess the performance of partnerships to identify areas for improvement and optimize outcomes. Maintain open lines of communication, address any issues or concerns proactively, and celebrate successes together to strengthen the partnership over time.

By building a powerful network of mentors, advisors, and collaborators, leveraging social capital for access to opportunities and resources, and establishing mutually beneficial partnerships and alliances, you can accelerate wealth creation and achieve greater success in your personal and professional endeavors.

Chapter 5: Risk Management and Resilience

Developing a Robust Risk Management Strategy to Safeguard Wealth and Minimize Losses:

Risk management is a critical aspect of successful investing and wealth preservation. A robust risk management strategy involves identifying, assessing, and mitigating potential risks to safeguard wealth and minimize losses.

Start by conducting a thorough risk assessment of your investment portfolio, considering factors such as market volatility, liquidity risk, geopolitical events, and regulatory changes. Identify potential risks and their potential impact on your financial goals and objectives.

Next, implement risk mitigation strategies to protect your wealth and minimize losses. This may include diversifying your investments across different asset classes, sectors, and geographic regions to spread risk and reduce exposure to any single risk factor.

Additionally, consider using hedging strategies such as options, futures, and derivatives to protect against downside risk and limit potential losses.

Maintain adequate liquidity to weather unexpected expenses or market downturns without needing to sell off assets at a loss.

Regularly monitor and reassess your risk exposure to ensure it remains aligned with your risk tolerance and investment objectives. Adjust your portfolio allocation and risk management strategies as needed to adapt to changing market conditions and economic environments.

Diversifying Investments and Maintaining a Balanced Portfolio:

Diversification is a cornerstone of sound investment strategy, allowing investors to spread risk and optimize returns by investing in a variety of asset classes with low correlation to one another.

To diversify your investment portfolio, allocate capital across different asset classes such as stocks, bonds, real estate, commodities, and alternative investments. Within each asset class, further diversify by investing in a mix of assets with varying risk profiles, industries, and geographic regions.

Maintain a balanced portfolio allocation that reflects your risk tolerance, investment goals, and time horizon. Regularly rebalance your portfolio to ensure it stays aligned with your target asset allocation and risk parameters.

Consider incorporating non-traditional assets such as gold, cryptocurrencies, and collectibles into your portfolio to further diversify and hedge against inflation, currency risk, and market volatility.

Cultivating Resilience and Adaptability to Navigate Market Fluctuations and Economic Challenges:

Resilience and adaptability are essential qualities for navigating market fluctuations, economic downturns, and unforeseen challenges.

Cultivate resilience by adopting a long-term perspective and focusing on your overarching financial goals rather than short-term fluctuations in market prices. Embrace volatility as an opportunity to buy low and sell high, rather than as a cause for panic or distress.

Develop a contingency plan for managing financial setbacks or unexpected expenses, such as job loss, medical emergencies, or economic downturns. Maintain an emergency fund with sufficient liquidity to cover three to six months' worth of living expenses to provide a financial safety net during difficult times.

Stay informed about current events, market trends, and economic indicators to anticipate potential risks and opportunities. Continuously monitor and adjust your investment strategy in response to changing market conditions and economic environments.

Seek professional advice from financial advisors, wealth managers, and other experts to gain perspective and guidance on navigating complex financial situations. Surround yourself with a supportive network of friends, family, and mentors who can provide emotional support and practical advice during challenging times.

By developing a robust risk management strategy, diversifying investments, and cultivating resilience and adaptability, you can navigate market fluctuations and economic challenges with confidence and safeguard your wealth for the long term.

Chapter 6: Continuous Learning and Growth

Embracing a Lifelong Learning Mindset to Stay Ahead in an Ever-Evolving Landscape:

In today's rapidly changing world, the ability to adapt and learn continuously is essential for staying relevant and competitive. Embracing a lifelong learning mindset involves recognizing that learning is a lifelong journey and committing to ongoing personal and professional development.

To cultivate a lifelong learning mindset, start by adopting a growth mindset—a belief that your abilities and intelligence can be developed through effort, practice, and learning. Embrace challenges, view failures as opportunities for growth, and seek out feedback to improve continuously.

Stay curious and open-minded, actively seeking out new knowledge, experiences, and perspectives. Keep abreast of industry trends, technological advancements, and best practices by reading books, articles, and research papers, attending conferences, and participating in online forums and communities.

Investing in Personal and Professional Development to Enhance Skills and Knowledge:

Investing in personal and professional development is essential for enhancing skills, expanding knowledge, and advancing your career or business endeavors. Take a proactive approach to self-improvement by identifying areas for growth and investing time and resources into developing those skills.

Set specific, measurable goals for your personal and professional development, breaking them down into actionable steps and milestones. Invest in relevant training, courses, workshops, and certifications to acquire new skills and knowledge that align with your goals and interests.

Seek out opportunities for hands-on experience and practical application of newly acquired skills. Volunteer for projects, join professional associations, and take on leadership roles to gain valuable experience and demonstrate your capabilities to others.

Build a personal learning network of mentors, coaches, and peers who can provide guidance, support, and accountability as you pursue your development goals. Regularly seek feedback from trusted advisors and mentors to identify areas for improvement and refine your development strategy accordingly.

Leveraging Online Courses, Workshops, and Mentorship Programs for Continuous Growth and Improvement:

Online courses, workshops, and mentorship programs offer convenient and accessible avenues for continuous growth and improvement. Take advantage of these resources to learn new skills, gain insights from experts, and connect with like-minded individuals from around the world.

Research and select high-quality online courses and workshops that cover topics relevant to your personal and professional development goals. Look for courses offered by reputable institutions, instructors with relevant expertise and experience, and positive reviews from past participants.

Participate actively in online courses and workshops, engaging with course materials, completing assignments, and participating in discussions to maximize learning outcomes. Take advantage of supplementary resources such as webinars, podcasts, and online forums to deepen your understanding and connect with fellow learners.

Seek out mentorship opportunities with experienced professionals who can provide guidance, advice, and support as you navigate your personal and professional journey. Look for mentors who have achieved success in areas you aspire to and are willing to share their knowledge, insights, and experiences with you.

By embracing a lifelong learning mindset, investing in personal and professional development, and leveraging online courses, workshops, and mentorship programs, you can continuously grow and improve, staying ahead in an ever-evolving landscape and unlocking new opportunities for success and fulfillment.

Chapter 7: Giving Back and Impactful Philanthropy

Recognizing the Importance of Giving Back to Society and Making a Positive Impact:

Giving back to society and making a positive impact is not only a moral obligation but also a key component of a fulfilling and purpose-driven life. Recognizing the interconnectedness of humanity and the importance of contributing to the well-being of others can bring immense personal satisfaction and fulfillment.

Philanthropy goes beyond financial donations; it encompasses acts of kindness, volunteering, and advocacy for social causes. By giving back, individuals can address societal challenges, empower marginalized communities, and create positive change in the world.

Incorporating Philanthropy into Wealth-Building Strategies for Long-Term Fulfillment and Legacy:

Incorporating philanthropy into wealth-building strategies adds depth and meaning to financial success, providing a sense of purpose and fulfillment beyond monetary wealth alone. By aligning wealth-building efforts with philanthropic values and goals, individuals can create a lasting legacy that extends far beyond their lifetime.

Integrating philanthropy into financial planning involves setting aside a portion of income or assets for charitable giving, establishing donor-advised funds or charitable trusts, and incorporating charitable giving into estate planning strategies.

Consider creating a philanthropic mission statement or vision that reflects your values, passions, and desired impact. This will guide your philanthropic efforts and ensure that your charitable giving is aligned with your personal values and goals.

Supporting Causes Aligned with Personal Values and Contributing to Meaningful Social Change:

When selecting causes to support through

philanthropy, it's essential to consider issues that resonate deeply with your personal values, passions, and beliefs. Whether it's education, healthcare, environmental conservation, or social justice, choose causes that align with your values and where you can make a meaningful impact.

Research nonprofit organizations, charities, and social enterprises that are making a difference in your chosen cause area. Evaluate their mission, programs, impact, and financial transparency to ensure that your donations will be used effectively and responsibly.

Consider leveraging your skills, expertise, and resources to support causes beyond financial contributions. Volunteer your time, serve on nonprofit boards or advisory committees, or use your influence to advocate for policy change and social justice.

Engage your family, friends, and professional network in philanthropic activities to amplify your impact and inspire others to give back. By mobilizing collective resources and efforts, you can create a ripple effect of positive change in your community and beyond.

In summary, giving back and engaging in impactful philanthropy is an integral part of wealth-building and personal fulfillment. By recognizing the importance of making a positive impact, incorporating philanthropy into wealth-building strategies, and supporting causes aligned with personal values, individuals can leave a lasting legacy of generosity, compassion, and social change.

Chapter 8: Scaling Success and Multiplying Impact

Scaling Successful Ventures and Expanding Wealth-Building Strategies for Exponential Growth:

Scaling successful ventures involves expanding operations, increasing market reach, and replicating proven business models to achieve exponential growth and maximize returns on investment. To scale successfully, entrepreneurs must identify scalable opportunities, optimize processes, and secure adequate resources for growth.

Identify opportunities for scaling by analyzing market demand, customer feedback, and competitive landscape to identify areas for expansion and growth. Develop a scalable business model that can accommodate increased demand, production, and distribution without compromising quality or efficiency.

Invest in infrastructure, technology, and human capital to support scaling efforts. Expand distribution channels, invest in marketing and advertising, and optimize supply chain management to reach new markets and customer segments.

Monitor key performance indicators (KPIs) and metrics to track progress and identify areas for improvement. Continuously iterate and optimize business processes, products, and services to ensure scalability and sustainability over the long term.

Multiplying Impact Through Innovative Business Models, Investments, and Philanthropic Initiatives:

Multiplying impact involves leveraging resources, expertise, and influence to create transformative change and address systemic challenges facing society. By adopting innovative business models, making strategic investments, and supporting philanthropic initiatives, individuals and organizations can amplify their impact and create lasting social change.

Explore innovative business models such as social enterprises, impact investing, and shared value initiatives that align financial success with social and environmental impact. By integrating social and environmental objectives into core business strategies, companies can generate positive returns for shareholders while addressing pressing societal issues.

Make strategic investments in organizations, projects, and initiatives that have the potential to create significant social, environmental, or economic impact. Consider investing in social enterprises, clean energy projects, affordable housing initiatives, or education programs that address systemic challenges and improve quality of life for underserved communities.

Support philanthropic initiatives that address root causes of social problems and create sustainable solutions. Invest in capacity-building, advocacy, and policy change efforts that address systemic inequalities, promote social justice, and empower marginalized communities to thrive.

Empowering Others to Achieve Financial Independence and Become Millionaires Through Education, Mentorship, and Empowerment:

Empowering others to achieve financial independence and become millionaires involves sharing knowledge, providing support, and creating opportunities for others to succeed. By offering education, mentorship, and empowerment programs, individuals can help others overcome barriers to success and achieve their full potential.

Offer financial literacy education and entrepreneurship training to equip individuals with the knowledge and skills they need to manage their finances, start businesses, and build wealth. Provide mentorship and guidance to aspiring entrepreneurs, sharing insights, experiences, and lessons learned from your own journey to success.

Create opportunities for economic empowerment through job training programs, vocational education, and workforce development initiatives that provide individuals with the skills and resources they need to access stable employment and achieve financial security.

Promote diversity, equity, and inclusion in entrepreneurship and wealth-building initiatives by actively supporting underrepresented groups, minority-owned businesses, and women entrepreneurs. Provide access to capital, networking opportunities, and mentorship programs that level the playing field and create pathways to success for all.

By scaling successful ventures, multiplying impact through innovative business models and philanthropic initiatives, and empowering others to achieve financial independence through education, mentorship, and empowerment, individuals can create a ripple effect of positive change and build a more inclusive and prosperous society for future generations.

Conclusion: Empowering the Masses to Millionaire Status

In conclusion, achieving millionaire status is within reach for anyone willing to adopt the right mindset, implement strategic wealth-building strategies, and embrace a lifelong commitment to learning and growth. Throughout this guide, we have explored key strategies and principles for rapid wealth accumulation, empowering individuals to unlock their full potential and create a legacy of abundance and prosperity.

Recap of Key Strategies and Principles for Rapid Wealth Accumulation:

1. Cultivate a mindset of abundance, determination, and strategic thinking. Embrace the belief that wealth is attainable and commit to taking consistent, purposeful action towards your financial goals.
2. Leverage technology to streamline wealth generation, optimize investment strategies, and explore new opportunities for growth, such as cryptocurrency, blockchain, and decentralized finance (DeFi).
3. Invest strategically in diverse asset classes, identify high-potential investment opportunities, and implement income-generating strategies to maximize returns and minimize risk.
4. Build a powerful network of mentors, advisors, and collaborators, leveraging social capital for access to opportunities, resources, and knowledge.
5. Develop a robust risk management strategy, diversify investments, and cultivate resilience and adaptability to navigate market fluctuations and economic challenges.

6. Embrace a lifelong learning mindset, investing in personal and professional development to enhance skills and knowledge continuously.
7. Incorporate philanthropy into wealth-building strategies, supporting causes aligned with personal values and contributing to meaningful social change.
8. Scale success and multiply impact by expanding successful ventures, investing in innovative business models and philanthropic initiatives, and empowering others to achieve financial independence through education, mentorship, and empowerment.

Encouragement to Take Action, Persevere, and Seize Opportunities for Financial Success:
Now is the time to take action, persevere through challenges, and seize opportunities for financial success. Remember that wealth accumulation is a journey, not a destination, and success requires dedication, discipline, and resilience.

Stay focused on your goals, remain adaptable to change, and never lose sight of your vision for financial freedom and abundance. Trust in your abilities, seek out opportunities for growth, and surround yourself with a supportive network of mentors and peers who can inspire and guide you along the way.

Vision for a Future Where Millions Achieve Millionaire Status and Create a Legacy of Abundance and Prosperity:

Imagine a future where millions of individuals worldwide achieve millionaire status, not only for their own financial gain but also to create a legacy of abundance and prosperity for future generations. In this future, wealth is not hoarded but shared generously to uplift communities, support meaningful causes, and create a more equitable and inclusive society.

By empowering the masses to achieve millionaire status and embracing a collective vision of abundance and prosperity, we can create a world where everyone has the opportunity to thrive and make a positive impact on the world. Together, let us work towards this vision and build a brighter, more prosperous future for all.

To you, the future millionaire,

I extend my heartfelt gratitude for embarking on this journey with me through the pages of "Accelerated Millionaire: The Ultimate Guide to Rapid Wealth." Your decision to invest in your financial future is commendable, and I am honored to be a part of your quest for success.

As you delve into the wealth of knowledge contained within these pages, know that you hold the keys to unlocking your fullest potential and achieving unparalleled success. May each chapter serve as a beacon of inspiration and guidance, lighting the path to prosperity and abundance.

On your rapid path to wealth, may you encounter countless opportunities for growth, learning, and transformation. May you navigate challenges with grace, courage, and resilience, emerging stronger and more empowered than ever before.

Above all, I wish you abundance in all areas of your life—abundance of wealth, abundance of joy, and abundance of fulfillment. May "Accelerated Millionaire" be the catalyst that propels you towards your dreams, allowing you to live a life of purpose, passion, and prosperity.

Here's to your continued success and abundance on your journey to becoming an Accelerated Millionaire.

With gratitude and best wishes,

Casey Kroon

The Only Person that will make you a millionaire is you.

And it will start once you choose to take action steps along that path.

There are many paths to the top of the mountain. Which path will you take?

Start today, right now, this minute. All we have is the now and the choice to act or be in it. Tomorrow isn't a real destination. Become your best self. Start now.

www.ingramcontent.com/pod-product-compliance
Lightning Source LLC
Chambersburg PA
CBHW070417230526
45471CB00006B/2857